My Hero is M.O.M
"Made Of Melanin"

Musings by Regina Elaine

Regina Elaine

First paperback edition March 2026

Book design by Goga Design Lab

ISBN 979-8-2340-1926-4 (paperback)
Library of Congress Control Number: 2026905868

Published by Alphagraphics Campbell
Phoenix, AZ
us011.alphagraphics.com

Poetic Pieces…

Musings: thoughtful, reflective, and often written expressions or meditations on topics ranging from daily life to deep philosophical questions.

FOREWORD

Foreword:

This project is a multidirectional, poetic tribute turned into a book—a collection of lyrical odes, poetic pieces, and intimate narrative moments illuminating motherhood's rich, layered experience. These poems speak in many directions: as a mother, daughter, and woman. Each piece is deeply personal yet intentionally universal, designed so that Black mothers everywhere can feel seen, honored, and celebrated for who they are, what they carry, and all that they give.

At the heart of this project is the recognition that being a mom is not separate from being a woman—it is, in fact, deeply intertwined. The woman becomes a mother, but she never ceases to be a woman. Her dreams, her softness, her fire, her identity—these do not disappear in motherhood; they evolve. This book seeks to explore that intersectionality, that sacred and sometimes tension-filled overlap between nurturing others and needing nurture, between giving life and claiming one's own. It honors the duality, the balancing, the sacrifice, and the becoming.

This is not just a book—it's an emotional experience. Personally designed it will feel like art in your hands. Each page turns like a portal into a moment—with musings, a memory, a feeling, a reflection, a prayer. The aesthetic will complement the lyrical and emotional complexity, and our generational power rhythm of the text, enhancing its impact and offering a tactile sense of reverence.

M.O.M., standing for *Made Of Melanin*, is a love letter to Black mothers. It is an ode to our strength, our beauty, our power. Through themes of motherly love, resilience, cultural pride, and emotional depth, the book will echo the voices of Black women who mother with unmatched grace and grit, whether quietly or loudly, visibly or invisibly.

This project is for every Black mother who's ever felt unseen. For every Black woman carrying the legacy of the women who mothered her. For every daughter who is now a mother, still figuring out how to hold both roles. It is a rhythmic, emotionally rich, and visually striking tribute to all that we are: women, mothers, daughters—*Made of Melanin*.

This book is created with Black moms in mind. While I honor and celebrate all mothers, this project is a tribute to the women who reflect who I am, where I draw inspiration, who I admire, who surround me, and who I've shared the parenting journey with throughout my life.

I'm thinking of the young moms and the seasoned ones. The grandmothers, the grandmothers stepping back in as moms. The sports moms, the always-on-the-go moms, and the quieter ones who love just as fiercely. The moms who show up in every way possible—who go hard in the paint for their children, day in and day out.

This book is a celebration of *us*. A lyrical experience rooted in authenticity, love, and pride.

Tribute: a gesture, gift, speech, or act intended to show respect, admiration, gratitude, or esteem for someone.

WHAT IS A CHILD?

What is a Child?

PROLOGUE:

"What is a child" is a poem I wrote shortly after I had my first child. (25+ years ago!)

It is the first time that I expressed any raw emotion out loud about being a mom

A child is ...

To be nurtured, hugged, and held tight

Read a story, kissed and told "I love you" every night

A child is ...

Innocence, a gift from above

A precious miracle, a child is love

A child ...

Holds your heart and should be handled with care

NOT abused or abandoned, BUT shown off everywhere

A child is …

YOU, a reflection both good and bad

So, when your child is showing out, it’s just YOU, don’t get mad

A child is …

To be taught

Teach them strength, humor, and how to be bold

Most importantly, teach them responsibility

They may have to take care of you when you get old

A child is …

Your greatest challenge, BUT

Things will be alright, you’ll see,

You're a good person, and a child is what you used to be

Raw Emotions: intense, immediate feelings that surface after a significant event.

MY HERO IS MADE OF MELANIN

My Hero is Made Of Melanin

The day I was born, I was small and mighty

Mom was there, taking care of me

With gentle hands and loving eyes

Her pride and joy, I was the ultimate prize

Through laughter and tears

Wiping my face, holding my hand

Teaching me to walk

Her face gleams when I stand

My champion, she beams with pride

Cherishing her little one, her heart opened wide

Skin like the earth, rich and deep

With a soul so strong, and a heart that speaks

Always there through thick and thin

My hero is Mom, Made Of Melanin

Packing lunches, she smothers me with kisses

Keeping me safe, praying there's nothing she misses

Through trials and tribulations, she remains standing tall

Staying strong through my stumbles, lifting me when I fall

She cheers me on and calms my fears

Believes in me and wipes away my tears

From golden dawn to a dark midnight hue

Her melanin shines, no matter the view

It is in her color, her radiance, her speech, her tones

This woman has magic flowing through her bones

Showing in her face, and the shine of her skin

My hero is Mom, like no other; she's Made Of Melanin

With hands made for healing and words that soothe

She is a source of love and prays that life stays smooth
Not for gold or fame,
Not even for a name.
Raising me to live proudly, with no regrets, and no shame

Her love is fierce, her strength is true,
She is my guiding light in all I do.
She has always been there, from the time I was small
My hero is Mom, Made Of Melanin
Her love outshines all

Molding my very soul
To be a decent human…is the plan, the ultimate goal
Protection from negative energy… it is everywhere, flowing freely
Shielding me from empty advice and noise,
"Don't choke on bad air," she says—"rise above it, rejoice."

Avoid the shallow, empty chatter,
Stand up tall and rise—it doesn't matter.

She pours from her spirit, always giving more
A heart so big, as if a wide-open door
Her love is a gift, an endless outpour

While I may go down, I'll always rise back up
My hero is Made Of Melanin, she will never give up
She feeds my self-esteem, she keeps my future bright
She raises me to be a warrior
I know I will be alright

My hero stands tall with a radiant glow,
A legacy deep, like rivers that flow.
Strength in her stride, fire in her eyes,
Lifting dreams, reaching past the skies.

Roots strong like the tallest of trees,

Carrying history with every breeze

A beauty so bold, so fierce from within

My hero is Mom, Made of Melanin

Through struggle and storms, she will never retreat,

Turning pain into power, rising in heat.

Voice like thunder, heart full of grace,

Shaping the world, reclaiming her space.

From past to present, her greatness remains,

Etched in the earth, like unshaken chains

A warrior, a leader, a light that won't dim.

My hero is Mom, Made Of Melanin

A crown she wears, a light so rare

With a hug and a smile, she always shares
She is a legend rising, bold and unbound,
Walking with pride, steadfast and profound

So when I stand, when I dare to dream,
I see her shining, a brilliant beam.
My hero, my guide, my strength within
It will always be my Mom, she is pure, Made Of Melanin

Hero: a person admired for courage, outstanding achievements or noble qualities often risking themselves for the common good.

There is MORE to say…

There is MORE to say: A Message to My Daughters

This piece is a love letter to my daughters and every Black girl navigating a world that often tries to shrink her light. These are the words I want my girls to hear, hold, and carry with them.
Wisdom whispered, guidance gifted, love spoken out loud. This is for you.

As a Black mom of daughters,

there are so many things that I want to tell my daughters,

say to my daughters,

share with my daughters.

But there is always something more to tell, to say, and to share.

It seems so simple,

but nothing is, really.

My message to our girls is here—

wrapped in too many words...

a mystery.

Our girls.

My girls.

Any Black girl here in any shared space.

Messages spoken in code, online,

nothing told face to face.

What I want my girls to know—

Here goes...

Lay down your defenses.

Listen.

Pay attention to your senses.

Hold space there, wherever you are.

Make conscious choices.

Slow your moves,

but keep going—

Far.

Past where you can even imagine.

Where you dare to dream.

Set your sights on a future.

See past what's in front of you.

See things that may not even seem...

Possible.

Listen with your heart, with your ears, with your mind.

Hold onto words that speak to you—

like a treasure you were blessed to find.

Discard what you don't.

Negative vibes? Push them away.

Keep safe what you need.

Count your blessings every day.

Stop and smell the roses.

Embrace the new experience.

Learn your lessons with humility.

Shut out arrogance.

Remember:

Behavior equals consequences.

There is no avoiding it.

No safety fences.

Life keeps moving—

learn and grow.

It seems to be that simple,

like that's all you need to know.

But there is more.

More to know,

more to say.

Lend me your ear,

while I give you a few more directive words

that will light your path,

making it easier to find your way.

Guard your SPIRIT.

It is the essence of you—

a reflection of who you are.

Let me break it down so you know

how your spirit makes you a superstar:

Strong

Positive

Inspirational

Real

Intelligent

Talented

That's it.

Together they are **DOPE**,

but individually they are the **SHIT**.

Standing Strong

Strength is not always found in your ability to speak up.

Sometimes, strength is knowing when to shut up.

Staying Positive

Positivity is not always a smile.

Sometimes, it's found in acceptance and growth—

knowing that simply growing up is how you show up,

and stay up.

Being Inspirational

Inspiration is not always *what* you see.

It can be *how* you see.

Keeping it Real

Real is not the same for everyone.

Your reality may be different—

so in keeping it real,

remember to respect the humanity of others.

Showing Intelligence

Intelligence is not always what you know.

It can be admitting that you do **not** know.

Owning Your Talent

Talent is not always doing something well.

It can be teaching someone else how to do something well.

You get it?

You feel me?

Was the message felt?

There is more.

I'm going to tell you how it's okay.

And this part—this part is heartfelt:

It's okay **not to know**,

but you gotta find out.

It's okay **not to like**,

but find out what you *do* like.

It's okay **to change your mind**,

but regroup, decide, and commit.

It's okay **to fall**,

but you gotta get back up.

But still…

There is more.

You are kind of a big deal.

If you are hurt along the way,

allow yourself time to heal.

Accept it.

Process it.

And move on.

Allow yourself **grace.**

Life is happening in real time.

There is no try-on.

Don’t chase people—**anyone.**

You are here.

You are important.

Don't get caught up in idle foolishness and simple chatter.

You do not need to run after anyone to prove anything.

Know this:

You are enough.

And that is all that should matter.

SPIRIT: the essence of a person, you as a human. It is not what you are but who you are; the seat of emotions and character, your soul. The real you is found in that part of you that is not physical. It is your values, your memories, your habits, your personality, your sense of humor.

AND then there was EVEN MORE to say…

And THEN there was EVEN MORE to say:
These are words to recognize those of us who were raised "ole school," the extra strength needed for the moms I know who have had children die, and the different strength needed for the moms of teens.

To my old-school mommas, I've got something to say—
I know how you get down, strong every day.
Check it...

That look? Stops you dead in your tracks.

No words, no movement—just that side-eye attack.

One brow raised, a slow head shake,

You know what that means, so you really start to quake.

Sunday mornings? Let the hair wars begin—

Hot comb sizzlin', burning edges, burning skin.

"Don't flinch. Sit still." Then *POP* goes the brush,

Blue grease, heavy hands, and always in a rush.

Every store run? A whole field trip, okay?

"Don't touch nothin'" is the anthem we play.

Run into a friend? Oh Lord—settle in...

"Girl, how's your mama? Your fam? That little friend?"

House slipper—weapon. That flick? Too slick.
Before you blink, she handled it quick.
The belt? Yeah... we don't gotta go there.
Just know Mom's reflexes? Unmatched. *Beware.*

Food seasoned so deep, ancestors cheer,
Mac and cheese, collards, fried chicken near.
Ask for McDonald's? Oh, what a crime—
"We got food at home, stop wastin' my time!"

Yet through it all, her love stands tall—
She prays, she guides, she carries it all.
The magic. The strength. The ultimate win.
She is my hero—Mom. Made Of Melanin.

Now I speak from a place soft and true,
Because, Mom, I know you're listening too.
This part is hard, so I tread with care,
Carried beneath your heart, love woven rare.

Dreams of laughter, hands to hold,
Stories whispered, futures told.
Time was brief; too soon, you flew—
A life cut short, but my love stays true.

No cries to soothe, no steps to chase,
Just echoes left in a hollowed space.
Your child's name etched in your soul,
Love unbroken, endlessly whole.

Though my arms are empty, my heart still knows—
A mother's love forever grows.
You were here—and here you stay,
In whispered winds and skies of gray.

In golden dawn, in stars that gleam,
In every tear, in every dream.
No time, no space, no silent grave
Can steal the love or joy you gave.

My heart, your heart—through grace and pain,

We are still one. I see your face again.

My strength within, your legacy begin—

Because you were Mom, proudly Made Of Melanin.

And now, to you, Mom, on this wild ride,

When your kid gets bold—thinks *they* decide.

What happened to that sweet little one?

One day they love you, the next day they're gone.

Eye rolls often, sighs even louder,

Attitude strong, the friend group louder.

Snacks? Gone. Charger? Missing.

"Mom, get out!" Like you don't need permission.

"Watch that tone!" you say, on repeat,

But they're scrolling, sighing, glued to their seats.

Laundry mountain—skyline view.

"Nothing to wear," but it's all brand new.

Fridge empty. Ain’t no food in sight.

"Can we DoorDash?" *With what money?* Right.

Mood swings quick, sass on demand,

But let ‘em need somethin’? It’s *you* they demand.

"Mom, can you drive me?" "Mom, I need cash!"

Oh now you exist? That switch-up is brash.

When life gets loud, and friends aren’t near,

It’s Mom they seek, ‘cause you're always here.

To hug them tight in your sacred space,

And in their eyes—you still see that baby face.

You raised her right, showed her the way,

With love that doesn’t shift or sway.

Through childhood scrapes and teenaged sighs,

She sees your soul through grown-up eyes.

Your baby’s grown, but still in your hands—

Your rock, your love, your heart—she stands.

You’re not just her mother, but her best friend too,

With a bond that time can’t undo.

You laugh, you sip, the tea you spill,

Side-eye sync? You’ve mastered that skill.

Her melanin glows—rich, divine,

A mirror of you, your strength, your shine.

Grace in her face, fire in her pace,

You cheer her on—she’s your safe space.

Through all the seasons, thick and thin,

You remain her hero—

You’re Mom, proudly Made Of Melanin

"S.E.L.F."

S*.trong*

E*.nough 2*

L*.ove myself*

F*.irst*

Legacy of her love

Legacy of Her Love

A mother makes a choice—

a decision of the heart.

She gives her children life,

planting good things...

that give their young lives their start.

The family begins with her,

one very important part of her social being.

She is the parent,

you are the child—

a bond of love that is never fleeting.

The family becomes you,

and defines who you are—

becoming your very existence,

guiding your path
like a shining star.

When the winds and rains of life come at you,
Mom protects you just enough—
allowing you room to grow,
so alone,
you can stand up
strong and tough.

A mother leads by example,
in the best way she knows—
teaching you morals
that shape you
as your wisdom grows.

You take these lessons—
they guide your way,

planting seeds of discernment
that flourish and stay.

Instilling strong values,
encouraging you to dream,
Mom fosters and nurtures—
growing your seeds
of self-esteem.

The family grows,
and though we live apart,
we are bound by blood
and joined at the heart.

Through different struggles,
we stand as one—
a lifeline unbroken,
never undone.

The family—

Mom's greatest achievement.

Children carry her legacy.

Honor her love.

Live your best life...

with pride

and integrity.

Small Moments...

Live Learn Grow

Strength is in your roots and

Roots can be repotted and regrown

Do not let experiences define you

The Voice of a Teenager

Prologue:
This piece was written during a time when my oldest daughter was a teenager. We all remember how crazy it is navigating the teenage years, big feelings, small voice. My daughter was doing well, and together we were mapping out her life's course and doing ok. Then, a coach who did not work directly with my daughter OR even knew my daughter, spoke ill of my daughter, implying that she could do so much better at this one aspect of her life (athletics) if she really applied herself and was more disciplined. My daughter was excelling at her sport. But I wanted to make sure that she had balance in her life while staying the course and navigating her teenage emotions, insecurities and normal hesitations. My goal was to take her into adulthood whole and not broken because I pushed her so hard in one area without taking into consideration all of the other areas of her life that mattered also. This piece is about the emotional complexities of being a teen, the many faces of a teenager.

The Voice of a Teenager

I am the VOICE of a teenager.

On a path of darkness with flashes of light at every bend—

ending on a curve…

I am confused.

I see you—holding a light,

guiding me through the fog.

But I'm prideful.

I'm stubborn.

I'm headstrong.

Still, I am embracing every role my living has created for me.

I am MORE than JUST a teenager.

Teenagers—are you out there?

Can I hear a voice?

I am a...

Dancer.

Therapist.

Cook.

Swimmer.

Babysitter.

Photographer.

Entrepreneur.

Maid.

Gymnast.

Wrestler.

I am the VOICE of a teenager

Please don't judge me.

I am living.

I am learning.

I am growing.

I'm just being the only me I know how to be.

I am smiling—

with tears rolling down my face,

leaning over the edge of emotional doom, falling into a sea

of mixed-up feelings.

I am confused.

But I see you—offering a shoulder,

an ear,

a tissue,

as I swim through.

I'm moody.

I've got an attitude.

But I'm building emotional strength.

I am MORE than JUST a teenager.

Teenagers—are you out there?

Can I hear a voice?

I am...

Nice.

Mean.

Jealous.

Spirited.

Caring.

Sensitive.

Playful.

Disciplined.

Tired.

Emotional.

Detached.

I work hard.

I study harder.

I am the VOICE of a teenager.

Please don't judge me.

I'm living.

I'm learning.

I'm growing.

I'm just being the only me I know how to be.

I'm in the driver's seat—

on an unfamiliar road

with no permit

and no map.

I am confused.

But I see you—

holding the handbook,

spreading out the map,

showing me how to get where I'm meant to grow.

I am living.

I am learning.

I am growing.

I am MORE than just a teenager.

Teenagers—are you out there?

Can I hear a voice?

I HEAR the voice of a teenager.

You are a student.

A brother.

A niece.

A cousin.

An athlete.

A mentor.

A protector.

A sister.

A friend.

I HEAR your voice, teenager.

Please don't judge me.

I'm just being the only me I now know how to be.

I am the VOICE of a teenager.

Not to be defined.

Not to be boxed in.

Not to be what YOU think I should be.

Not a mannequin—

for you to dress, mold, and pose.

I am a soldier for life—

and this life is MY boot camp.

I am living.

I am learning.

I am growing.

Please don't judge me.

I'm being the only me I know how to be.

Hear me.

I AM the VOICE of a teenager.

Know me?
Like me?
No.
Acknowledge me?
Recognize me?
Respect me?
Yes!!

The Soul of You

The Soul Of You

The soul of you

is **YOU**

at your deepest core.

It drives,

it thrives—

it's what you're living for.

Will you let in

all this negative air?

Listening to empty words,

just because they're there?

It's like choking on smoke

when you're meant to rise,

or drowning in inches

when you're built to climb high.

You are **strong**—

bend,

but never fold.

Let no burden

dim your soul's bright gold.

And though you may stumble,

always stand tall.

Protect your soul—

it's your power,

your all.

Rise above.

Let your light shine through.

Beautiful girl,

you were made to breakthrough

Find yourself . . . and be her.

Look inside yourself. . .be your own hero.

Beautiful as YOU are

Beautiful, as YOU are

Beautiful—

as **YOU** are,

and unapologetically so.

Nothing external

can dull your glow.

Thriving.

Striving.

Confident in your flow.

Your game is DOPE.

You are driven and determined,

label-less,

your aura is full...

Full of strength,

resilience,

promise,

and confidence.

Your game is FIERCE.

Be **extra.**

Be **bolder.**

Be **badder.**

Beautiful—

as **YOU** are.

Limitless.

Undefined.

Choices…

Choose to stay

Choose to leave

Choose to be content

Choose to just be

Your life, your choices

YOU, More than Enough

YOU, More Than Enough

Look at you, shining bright—
more than enough.
Grace in your stride,
got that **diamond-cut tough**.

Every step you take,
I'm watchin' in awe,
from the hurdles you clear
to the dreams you draw.

Wisdom in your eyes,
fire deep in your soul—
every page you write,
your story is **gold**.

You are the **main act**,
the **star**, never playin' it small.
I'm just here front-row,

watchin’

year after year of you,

givin' your all

You—

the one they all wanna be.

But they can’t copy your glow,

they can’t repeat your energy.

Built from love,

truth,

and so much more.

I’m **proud** of you.

You are everything **real**.

No amount of pain could break you—

it’s just how you’re built.

Shots taken, they tried,

but you are standin’ here still.

Royalty flows in your veins;

that's what makes you such a big deal.

Left dark shadows behind—

they can't dim what you do.

No rewriting the past,

just hard work and strong follow-through.

You built your path—

no permission needed.

Determination fueled you

when the odds had you defeated.

Taught to rise,

to lead,

to move,

to fight—

how to bloom through the storms,

with **beauty on sight**.

They could never comprehend

how you glow so true—

how you took broken pieces

and turned 'em all brand new.

YOU, More Than Enough cont'd

So keep risin', my love,

with that crown on your head.

Ain't nothing from your past

gonna haunt where you tread.

We the team,

we the truth,

let 'em talk if they dare—

'cause the love that you got

ain't for sale or compare.

So stand tall,

let 'em watch,

let ’em learn,

let ’em see—

You are the one.

You are the light.

You are the legacy.

Enough: not having to strive to become more worthy, valid, acceptable, or loved. You are already ALL of those things and more.

My Son, My Black Son

My Son, MY Black Son

Prologue:
Though I don't have sons of my own, this piece was born from a place of deep empathy.

During a family conversation about the heartbreaking number of Black men losing their lives, my youngest daughter suddenly broke down in tears—overwhelmed by fear for her father and the young Black boys she calls friends.

At that moment, I felt the weight that so many mothers carry.

This piece is written as a fictional letter to a son I don't have, but it's also a love letter—a tribute—to my sisters who are raising Black sons in a world that doesn't always see their brilliance, their beauty, or their humanity.

My son.
My son.
My Black son.

You wouldn't understand

unless you had one.

Stand tall. Be proud.

Don't be quiet,

but don't be *too* loud

Be assertive

speak your words, king

Have an opinion

Question everything

You have a voice

You deserve to be heard

Make them listen

Make them take you at your word

Your word is your bond

it may make others afraid

But remember

that's *their* fear to carry

That's not the bed you made

Brown. Castille. Garner. Rice. Floyd.

Names and feelings

married together

You can't avoid

I worry when you walk down the street

I worry about the people you meet

I worry that in expressing yourself

you'll be misunderstood

I worry that, no matter what you do

they still won't see the good

I want you to grow older

alive and intact

I want you to be *you*

without having to worry

about how you act

My son.

My son.

My Black son.

College. Career.

Meeting *The One*.

All this… and more

you deserve it all

But the real prize is your life

just living to receive a call.

Whether it's for a job interview,

a promotion,

or a friend asking for a ride to the mall.

I can't imagine what it's like—

to be hunted.

To be preyed

To be looked at and feared,

though there's no reason

to be afraid.

You are gentle.

You are kind.

You are smart.

You speak your mind.

Who are you…

What you'll be…

The whole wide world

deserves to see.

My Son.

My Black Son.

No matter how the world perceives,

or what the images project—

YOU have always been The One.

Pride: awareness of one's own dignity

My Everything

My Everything

You're my everything.

You are **everything** to me.

My sun,

my moon,

my stars—

my peace.

Your worth to me?

Beyond measure.

You inspire me

to a higher me,

to reach for more,

to rise,

to *be*.

No pain, no gain—

the pressure

was worth the pain.

Every tear became a lesson,

lessons learned became a blessing.

Every stumble made you shine.

Face forward—

no looking behind.

Your aura,

your strength,

your dignity...

shines through

so **brilliantly**.

Better you—

I expected of you.

Not for perfection,

but because I saw your *truth*.

To look,

to aim,

to **be the best of you**—

not for me,

but for everything

you're meant to do.

When the world pressed in,

you didn't fold.

You gathered grace

and turned it **bold**.

You pushed past fear,

through nights of doubt—

no matter the experience,

you always find your way *out*.

I've watched you bloom
through concrete and pain.
I've seen you fight,
and **rise again**.

You don't just walk—
you move the air.
A quiet storm
with power to spare.

Your voice,
your vision—
you control the room.

Improving yourself?
That's your only competition.
It's *you against you*—
meaning **YOU always win**.

So when you doubt,

or feel unmade,

just know:

You are

the light

I prayed.

My sun,

my moon,

my stars you'll be—

Forever

and always,

everything to me.

Worth: one's dignity and unique purpose.
Personal

Morning Affirmation

Morning Affirmation

When we are born,

we are all the same—

little bitty people

that are given a name.

We are so cute,

a little sight to see,

blooming into our true selves—

our parents' mini-me.

Then we get older

and start toddling around,

growing up fast,

in leaps and bounds.

So cute or handsome,

a true sight to see...

how amazing you are—

you being you,

and me being me.

Starting your journey,

you do what you're told.

You learn your way,

you venture out—bold.

So you make mistakes,

you stumble along the way.

You start losing yourself,

listening more

to what others say.

What you hear

may make you sad,

make you cry real tears.

Insecurities creep up,

and you begin to have new fears.

But then you think...

Who cares what they say?!

I am unique, I am different,

I am just fine—

in **my own way.**

And so it begins,

you start to see—

it's okay for **you** to be you,

and **me** to be me.

It's not just about

who you really are...

Look inside yourself—

it's what you truly see

that makes **you** you,

and makes **me** me.

Hey, don't worry

about what you are *not,*

just be happy

for what you've got.

You have your talents,

your skills, your personality—

that makes you *you,*

and I'm happy

just to be *me.*

Look at me with my friends,

but don't compare.

It's just not right,

it's just not fair.

My friends are awesome,

and that is what you see,

but they are who they are—

and I am **just me.**

My friends are great,

they're cool, I see—

but I'm great too!

Jeez…

it's nice just to be me

I only have one life,

and I'm gonna be

the **absolute best**

there is to be.

I will be fabulous,

I will be great—

just wait and see!

But no matter what I am,

no matter where I go,

no matter what I do...

I will always, always

be

Me

Affirmation: words or thoughts you repeat to yourself to build confidence, challenge negative thoughts and encourage positivity.

No Superwoman Here

NO Superwoman Here

Prologue:
I know the title *"My Hero is Made Of…"* might seem like a contradiction here—but stay with me.

The piece *"My Hero is Made of Melanin"* is a reflection of how our children see us as moms. To them, we're the go-to for advice, guidance, money, comfort—or just that quiet calm only a mother can offer.

This spoken word is for every mother who's ever shown up fully for her children, even while trying to hold herself together. It's a reminder: you can be everything your child needs *without* losing yourself in the process. You can pour into them—but only if your own cup stays full.

It's for my single moms, and also for the ones who are partnered—but still carrying the emotional load of parenting solo while their person figures it out. This is for you. Your strength, your softness, your melanin—it's all part of your power, period.

Showing up in every way
Loving them babies,
Inspired by them every day
At times broken and bruised,
A human with feelings—
Sometimes tired and confused

Wondering, where does the time go?

Curating your family's needs—how does she know?

Is it really only 24 hours

In a day that's ours?

Praying, planning, and thinking,

Hoping there is nothing missing

Doing what you can,

Pretending you got it right,

When all the while thinking,

Hmmm, this just might…

Going through the motions because the children need

Wishing there was an app or Maternal Indeed

No cape to be worn,

Just a woman torn

No S on her chest—

Just a woman doing her best

No superpowers to draw upon,

At times no partner to pass the baton

When unknown, we figure it out—

Not for accolades, not for clout.

Just so the children can have a chance

For a decent life, a childhood enhanced

Godmom, auntie, cousin, friend—

Sometimes moms are repped from a different end.

Offering guidance, making sure a child is seen,

Offering a safe space because sometimes life is not pristine

Loved from the heart,

Playing the needed part

No cape to be worn,

Just a woman torn

No S on her chest—

Just a woman doing her best

No superpowers to draw upon,

Doing what's needed as she was passed the baton

Balancing life

As a mom and a wife,

Taking care of home,

The kids, the husband—and sometimes work

Same 24 hours, never enough time,

Trying hard not to go berserk

Having a partner can be a blessing and a burden,

Finding time between meals and naps to do a little flirting

Exhausted and tired—sleep before your body hits the bed,

Your husband already settled with naughty thoughts in his head

You smile and you try to muster those feelings,

Praying you can so your body will be willing

Sometimes you can, but sometimes your body won't,

Worried about your marriage because you know some women will what another don't

Still, you rise with the sun and fall with the moon,

Carving out memories that grow up too soon

From packed lunches to lullabies in the dark,

Every action a prayer, every word leaves a mark

You're more than a title, more than a role—

You're the keeper of rhythm, the anchor, the soul

Even when you feel you're falling apart,

You're still the heartbeat, the sacred heart

Legacy lives in the lessons you teach,

In the moments when love is just out of reach

And yet you stretch, you bend, you give—

Not just to survive, but to truly live

One day they'll say, "She was always there,"

Not perfect, but present—love in every stare

And maybe one day, when your hands finally rest,

You'll see—you weren't just good, you were truly the best

So no cape to be worn, no myth to uphold,

Just a woman of strength—fierce, fearless, and bold

No S on her chest, but a heart made of gold,

Just a woman doing her best—her story, her soul

Power: ability to do or act; capability to do or accomplish something. Strength, force, authority or influence.

Strong Girl|Bold Woman

Prologue:

This piece is deeply personal.
It began with the tangled, sometimes contradictory emotions that come with simply being a woman. The complexity. The beauty. The weight.

I often tell my girls that it's okay to feel everything, and I guide them through four phases to navigate those emotions:
Accept it. Process it. Move on. Give yourself grace.
And if you need to—**start again.**

In that rhythm, they begin to understand what it means to be strong as a girl… and bold as a woman.

Strong girl, bold woman,

Forged in truth, not illusion

Unique in her fire,

But still—beautifully human

Expectations different, consequences the same,

Wishing to be addressed simply by her name

No titles, no labels, no extra weight,

No questions, no judgment, no unnecessary hate

Sitting in spaces, voices unheard,

Screaming loudly—no one hearing a word

Always reminded of the power between her legs,

Always proving the power between her ears

Walking through a sea of extremities,

Invalidating the many labels of complexities

Listen to hear

Some of the burdens we bear—

Analogies, if you will,

Explaining some of the reasons we have to heal

An unscripted story, unbound by page or pen,

A rhythm born of silence, rewritten now and then

Chapters twisted in whispers only moonlight dares to read,

Each line a quiet thunder, each pause a secret need

Beneath the inkless verses, where truth and myth align,

Lies a hidden message in the margins of her spine

Not every word spoken, not every path shown—

Shrouded in mystery, her essence is full-grown

She is an artist, a mother, a healer, a rebel,

A quiet builder of worlds

Separate or all at once—

Not recognized at first glance, but

When you see her, when you truly see her,

You feel her story long after she leaves the room

She is that woman!

A mess left from the night before—

Lipstick smudged on a wine-stained floor

Ashes of laughter, perfume in the air,

A storm of dreams tossed everywhere

Don’t sweep her up, don’t make her small,

She is not debris—She is positioned in a sprawl

The wind takes what chaos made,

She rises in fragments, fierce and unafraid

She lands where maps have yet to name,

In places built from untamed flame

Not broken—becoming—with every gust,

A woman reborn from scattered dust

She is a woman underestimated, dismissed, and

misunderstood—

Until she became the storm, they couldn’t ignore

She is not seeking arrival; she’s seeking truth

Her journey is art in motion

She is that woman!!

She walks a line drawn not feeling free me—

Too bold, she is a storm; too soft, she ceases to be

When she speaks, her voice is weighed,

Measured not in meaning, but in how it's portrayed

If she rises, sounding clear, standing tall and true,

They say she's lost the grace they once thought they knew

Too sharp, too loud—too much, they claim,

As if strength in her should come with shame

But if she whispers, holding in her fire,

Letting silence stretch like razor wire,

They call it poise, but read it frail—

A woman afraid, destined to fail

So she stays between echo and hush,

Carving power from every shiver and crush.

Neither weak nor hard, but wholly real—

A woman unlearning how not to feel

She is every woman who's ever spoken up and been called emotional,

The woman who has held her tongue to keep the peace,

The woman who has rehearsed her words not for clarity, but

for acceptability.

She is reclaiming her voice on her terms.

She is that woman!!

She walks through a world where she wears her worth,

Like armor forged from her own birth.

Confidence sharp, standards high—

Yet for some, that's a reason to deny

If she stands tall, proud in her own

They call her conceited, threatened by what she's shown

As if knowing her value is somehow a flaw,

As if strength is something to be withdrawn

If she shrinks, bending to their silent plea

She finds an open door, quietly knowing "it's not for me"

It’s a path that leads to quiet pain,
Where heartache falls like relentless rain

Abuse wears the mask of ‘love’ so well,
Mental scars deeper than words can tell
She is torn between what’s seen and what’s true—
For in her confidence, she is forced to choose

She is a woman standing at the crossroads
Of self-assurance and vulnerability,
Navigating a world that wants to break her when she is strong
And control her when she is weak

She is many things
A warrior, lover, protector, a healer—
A woman constantly reclaiming her space
Strong, silent,

Navigating a world that both demands her strength and

punishes her for it

She is that woman!!

She is a scale, unmarked by limit,

Weighed down with the world, yet she won’t quit

Each burden pressed upon her frame,

She rises again, unchanged, the same

She carries the weight that others can't see—

The silent load of what it means to be

Not broken by the heaviness, not lost in the cost,

For every ounce carried, she is never truly lost

She resets and recalibrates, with quiet grace,

Adjusting to the load, an endless race

She is the keeper, the holder, the silent strength—

Stretching farther than anyone would ever think

She is a woman who never stops,

Even when the weight grows too heavy to bear

She is a pillar—

One whose strength is not just in what she does,

But in how she sustains

She holds it together,

Often at the expense of her own needs

She is that woman!!

She is a hostess, welcoming the crowd,

Emotions swirl, both soft and loud

Uninvited guests sneak through the door—

No warning, no grace, just more and more

Joy dances close with anger's stare,

Sadness lingers, despair in the air

Fear takes a seat beside regret,

While hope's the one still trying to forget

She offers them all a place to stay—

A smile, a warmth, though she's feeling frayed

No security to bar the door—

Each guest arrives, but leaves her unsure

Yet they promise to return again—

Each emotion, a familiar friend

She greets them all, with patience untold—

The hostess to feelings, young and old

She is the keeper of her own inner world,

Hosting every emotion that comes her way,

No matter how unwelcome or intense

She is an emotional architect,

Holding space for her own emotional storm

While continuing to welcome life's ebb and flow

She is a woman who endures and nurtures,

Even when she's uncertain of what's coming next

She is that woman!!

Strong girl, bold woman,

Forged in truth, not illusion

Unique in her fire,

But still—beautifully human

She is a woman.

Beautiful as she is—

And unapologetically so

Nothing external can dull her glow

Thriving and striving every day, every moment,

Confident as she flows

She is full—

Full of strength, resilience, and confidence,

Full of drive and determination

Big and bad,

Fierce and free,

Rooted and rising,

Genuine and undefined—

Label-less, limitless,

Entirely her own.

Strength: mental and moral power, force, firmness or courage.

Strength is not always found in your ability to speak up
Strength can be found in knowing when to shut up

Positive is not always found in your ability to stay up
Positive can be found in your ability to accept things and grow from them

Inspiration is not always what you see
Inspiration can be how you see

Reality is not the same for everyone
Your reality can and will be different from everyone else's

Intelligence is not always about what you know
Intelligence can be admitting when you don't know

Talent is not always in your ability to do something well

Your talent can be teaching someone who doesn't know how to do something well

Live YOUR OWN life YOUR OWN way!!

Still A Woman

Still A Woman

Prologue:
This piece is simply a reflection of me, as a mom, and as a woman.
I felt it was important to show that beneath the calm, the strength, and sometimes even the appearance that I don't care… is someone who cares deeply.
Sometimes, *so* deeply, it doesn't always show.

Mostly in leggings,

or a stained t-shirt,

tired eyes blinking—

always seeming to work.

The carpool queen,

the lunchbox wrangler—

no one sees the woman

writing poems in her journal.

Her hair's in a bun,

half hope, half despair,

barely holding her crown—

there's still power there.

In grocery aisles,

she hums soft dreams,

behind each task,

a soul still beams.

She seems to have disappeared—

beneath the playroom tide,

but she's only shifted,

not set aside.

For every "Mommy!"

called from sleep,

she holds a truth

she gets to keep.

She's still the fire,

still the flame,

still that girl—

dancing, no fame, no name.

Still the curve,

the sway, the spark—

even when life feels

dim and dark.

She's still that woman

with songs to sing,

even if whispered

between laundry flings.

Still worthy of mirrors,

lipstick, and light—

not just lullabies

and thankless nights.

Don't let the leggings fool you,

or the car seat throne—

a queen, she walks quiet,

always in her zone.

And though the world sometimes forgets to see,

she is still

wild, whole,

and gloriously free.

A Black woman—bold, divine,

a walking legacy,

the whole bloodline.

She is her momma's prayers,

her strongest might,

she holds hope in her hips,

and success in her sight.

She wears history like gold,

shining in the sweat,

and when the world gets loud,
I know she ain't done yet.

Built from struggle,
bathed in grace,
she turns resistance
into her sacred space.

Her joy is protest.
Her rest is war.
Every breath she breathes—
a truth, a roar.

She is the echo
of frustration's cry,
she is that girl,
her family's reason why,
with her head held high.

She’s tired, yes—
but never done.
She makes magic
on the run.

Still finding time
to rise, to glow,
still showing her daughters
how legacy grows.

She may not get the flowers,
the breaks, the ease,
but best believe—
she moves like trees:
deep-rooted,
storm-tested,
ever true.

Still soft. Still strong.

Still breaking through.

Through every challenge, she rises and stands,

with a heart full of dreams and strength in her hands.

No matter the struggle, no matter the storm,

she keeps moving forward—still a woman, persistent and reborn.

Actions do not show themselves in the same way for everyone.

Be YOU … Your Own Way.

Cries

Cries

Prologue:
This piece was born from a moment that shook me—my daughter called me in tears during one of the hardest seasons of her life.

As a mother, it was heartbreaking to sit with her in that pain, knowing I couldn't fix it, couldn't carry it for her. I knew she had to go through it… that it was necessary for her growth. But that doesn't soften the ache a mother feels when her child is hurting.

Sometimes the hardest thing is not the crying—it's *not being able to stop the tears.*

When you hear the cries,

Piercing your heart

A piece of you dies,

Wishing you could take away their pain

Toss it to the sky

Far from their eyes.

Tears don't always come with bruises,

Sometimes they fall from silent losses,

Invisible hurts and harsh little truths

That spill in lunchroom corners and schoolyard booths.

Cries…

From

Scraped knees and dreams denied,

Not getting picked, or being picked apart,

Heartbreaks they don't yet have language for—

Sobs that soak your shoulder,

And whispers like,

"Why is the world colder?"

You want to hush it,

Rush in, fix it,

But

Sometimes pain must press

To stretch the spirit.

There's sun after the rain, you say—

They may not believe it that day,

You walk through the storm beside them still,

Hands steady like time,

Heart iron-willed.

Cries…

From

Low test scores and failed college classes

Sitting alone while happiness passes.

Heartache that echoes in late-night texts,

Breakups that leave the soul perplexed.

Exhaustion from doing it all too well,

Carrying futures they can't yet spell.

Cramps, headaches, and growing pains,

Feeling like effort goes down the drain.

Love doesn't always melt it away,

But it anchors the soul so they don't sway

You breathe through tantrums,

Sit through silence,

You speak peace when life feels violent

Cries…

Cries…

Life's lessons, lullabies.

Ten toes down

Past the pain

Straight to the shine

Your life is intricately aligned with mine.

Cry for the unfair,

Cry for the try-hard,

Cry when your life's joy breaks down into shards.

Remember this

Every tear you spill

Waters the roots of who you will be

And I—your mother—am the sun,

Warming the soil,

Till your strength blooms full.

So cry…

Cry if you must.

I'll be the hush that doesn't rush,

The lap, the light, the lullaby,

The echo that answers every *why*—

Not always with reason,

But always with love.

Some storms are meant to be survived,

So you can learn that you are fire,

Not just fragile.

And on the other side,

You'll find the shine.

And I’ll be there—

Still listening.

Still here.

Every time…

You cry.

Every new experience is a tool, so live and continue to add tools to your toolbox. Just like you get rid of tools you don't need. If an experience is not something you like, simply discard the tool, pick up your toolbox and keep it pushing.

Rise, NOT Apologize

Rise, NOT Apologize

Quick to apologize and fail to rise.

Quick to apologize but slow to rise.

Another's perspective, understanding, or lies

Should not be your reason to apologize.

Accepting the error of your ways should be a lesson

A time to course correct, no time for deflection.

Rise above it and be a better person.

Learn from it. Earn from it. Don't burn from it.

Losing pieces of you each time you say "sorry"

For something that was never your story

Signing for a debt that isn't yours to pay

Carrying a shame that was never in your way

Your life holds weight just by being lived

Black, woman, born, already twice dismissed.

Refuse weight that was never yours.

Don’t let false guilt intensify your wars

Bending just to keep the peace,

Apologizing quick so the conflict will cease

Not every silence is noble or wise

Sometimes silence is how the truth dies

Shrinking yourself to soothe their pride.

Please, do NOT dim your fire allowing darkness for them to

hide

Apologies are sacred, not a reflex move

Coming from a place of truth, not a need to prove.

Your ‘sorry’ should not be a blanket or shield

Don’t kneel for battles where you weren’t meant to yield

Truths will sting, and some won’t be heard

Let your silence speak louder than your words.

You are not responsible for their discomfort.

Not every reaction deserves your remorse.

You carry you, as one, you walk with grace

Do NOT allow the guilt of others to alter your pace

Being Black being woman is already a stand

Already a storm, already a brand.

So carry what's yours, nothing more.

Leave their guilt outside their door

Some will guilt you just to feel tall,

To project their flaws, they are waiting for your fall

Stand firm, don't feed into their game.

Their shame is theirs, do NOT let it affect your name

Apologies without cause are chains in disguise.

They bind your truth, they blur your beautiful skies.

Discernment is power; learn when to speak,

Learn when silence makes you unique.

You are not difficult for demanding respect,

Not arrogant for choosing to protect

Your spirit, your joy, your God-given light—

You owe no one to dim who you are, to make their world bright.

Accept responsibility for your actions
Be accountable for your results
Take ownership of your mistakes

Accountability breeds responsibility

Accountability
It is not only what we do, It is also what we do not do for which we are accountable.

Evolution: Twisted Pieces

Evolution: Twisted Pieces

From splinters, come twisted pieces
Born in a storm
Humming lullabies during the day
goodnights in silence
sounding a lot like *go away.*

Mama was soft thunder,
wrapped in steel wool.
holding her babies like fine china
forgetting that even porcelain
needs space to breathe.

She loved like a wildfire
warm and controlled until it wasn't.
Gentle palms when they crawled,

tight fists when they stood.

She knew

lullabies but not listening

sacrifice but not surrender

hugs like armor,

BUT

only if you weren't too loud

too honest

too proud

too big

too much…of yourself.

a home built from the scraps of her childhood

walls of apology

roof of regret,

floors that creaked with the weight

of never being enough.

Still, she smiled.

Even when she cracked like old paint

and cried in corners when no one was looking

She was *Mother.*

Capital M.

Matriarch and Martyr

Feeding tiny souls with recipes she never got,

hoping her seasoning of survival would taste like love.

when her babies grew wings,

she clipped them out of habit

Not hate

unadulterated hesitancy and fear

How do you raise freedom

When fear has kept you in chains?

She couldn't braid boundaries into their hair.

Couldn’t thread safety into their clothing

But she tried.

she really *tried.*

With every story she told too late.

Every apology wrapped in silence.

Every “I love you” is buried in control.

Now she is Grandma

softened but scarred.

Kisses like caramel,

but shadows still in her sugar

Rocking the next generation

with calloused hands,
singing songs while still learning the words

Breaking generational curses
not cleanly
Not without blood or breakdowns
cracks in the dam.
New rivers running

But her children,
shaped from her contradictions
building bridges with bricks she never had.
They speak what she could not, feel what she feared.
They move through the world, whole-ish,
patched in places,
stitched with prayers and cloaked with their pain.

They are proof:

that even from splinters,

twisted pieces can present strong

Evolution: the process by which something new develops from something preexisting through successive growth and development.

Becoming: A Whole Built from Pieces

Becoming: A Whole Built from Pieces

For the daughter of the storm

raised

in the greenhouse of her grief

watered by warning,

sun-starved by silence,

still expected to bloom

as if she doesn't need light.

She gave love

like

a lesson.

a ledger.

a line to walk.

Taught me that hugs had hidden costs,

and freedom wasn't free

payments in pieces of your soul

She carries

her own broken mother

in her mouth

and her spine

speaking her name in anger,

wearing her shadow like perfume.

Promising to be her better.

Her do over

Her chance to do it right.

Wondering, questioning with sighing

silently asking

if she ever loved herself.

I became a mirror

she didn’t want to look into.

Reflected pieces

she buried deep

under "I’m fine"

and "You don't know what I've been through."

And maybe I didn’t.

But I *felt* it—

in the cracked tone of her praise,

the tension tucked behind every “I said so,”

in the way she called my softness weakness

and my strength rebellion.

I bled beneath the bandages of her past.

Fought for air

under the weight of her, unhealed.

But I …

chose evolution

Chose change

turning legacy

into leverage

Pain

into poetry.

stitching myself together

with borrowed joy,

therapy sessions,

nightly sobs

vowing my children would not hear

the echoes of the emotional chaos that raised me.

I became the voice

that answered the questions

she never dared ask.

I chose hugs without hesitation,

"No" without guilt,

"Yes" without condition.

My home built

with transparency and tenderness,

open doors

and open arms,

knowing wholeness isn't about being unbroken—

it's about *knowing where you cracked,*

and loving the light that shines through.

Now I watch my children dance

with a wholeness I never knew.

freedom ringing in their laughter.

Watering their truth

without fear

still her daughter.

shaped by her storm.

But I am also the calm.

The rebuild.

The rebirth.

I am becoming

not perfect,

but *present.*

A whole born from pieces.

Proof

that bloodlines don't have to be binding.

That roots can tangle

and still grow tall.

That from the splinters

twisted pieces hold value

and from storms

flowers bloom

Becoming: the process of growth and transition from who they are into who they are developing into. Stepping into the realization of one's value, worth, and possibilities.

The Best of Me

The Best of Me

The best of me

The only parts I see

Sacrificed my flaws

So you can have it all

Only the best parts

Not the baggage

my whole heart

Able to be

The best that you see

The better part of me

my faults,

my flaws,

my missteps in the dark—

they are my light,

my redemption

wrapped in their brilliance,

wide eyes full of knowing,

laughter that heals wounds

never spoken aloud

They walk with pieces of me I never celebrated,

grace where I carried grit,

hope where I once held hush.

Whole beings in the making,

with confidence too sacred for the world to steal—

carrying the best of me

my strength without the scars,

my softness without apology,

my dreams given legs

and edges

and wings.

When they rise,

I rise

Every smile,

a verse I didn't know I could write.

Every triumph,

An entry stitched from my silent regrets.

Every day,

they are the legacy I never knew I was building—

black girl magic

rooted in my name,

but reaching

far beyond what I could ever be, what I could ever see

The best of me

Various “fun” titles to describe ones self on this MOM journey:

- Decider of Discipline
- Mistress of Madness
- Master of Mayhem
- Coordinator of Chaos
- In the Moment Master of Madness
- Princess of Pennies
- Quintessential Queen of Quagmire

**Dedication and Gratitude

First and foremost,
Autumn and Haila — the two beautiful young women who made me a mother.

You are my heart walking around in the world. In you, I see the beauty of becoming, the power of presence, and the magic of unconditional love. Even in the moments when I felt like I was failing — as a mom, as a woman, as a human — your love and trust pulled me through. You reminded me, simply by believing in me, that I could not only survive but thrive.

Through trials and tribulations, open communication, and the never-ending work of love and growth, you have shown me what it means to rise. You remain my greatest accomplishment, my proudest achievement, and the very purpose that fuels my days.

You teach me, every single day, how important it is to show up — fully, fiercely, and authentically. Because of you, I continue to strive to be the best version of myself.

This book would not exist without your belief in me, your trust in my heart, and your place at the center of my soul. My love for you is infinite, immeasurable, and eternal.

With everything in me,
Mom

To my husband, **Larry** —
You are my quiet strength and unwavering support, the steady presence who held space for this dream without needing to say a word. Thank you for believing in me, for standing by me, and for being my greatest cheerleader — always, and in all things.

To my **father** —
Though you are no longer here to witness this moment, I feel your presence in every step of this journey.
I carry your love, your lessons, and your quiet strength with me always. I know that if you were able to be here, you would be — with pride in your eyes and warmth in your heart. Your absence is deeply felt, but your influence is ever-present. This book carries a piece of you, too.
Thank you for being a part of me, then, now, and always.

To my **mom** —
You taught me what to do, and — just as powerfully — what not to do. In both, you shaped me. In all, you gave me what I needed not just to be a great mom, but to be *me*.

To my **mother-in-law** —
Thank you for bringing your brand of love, support, and example. Your part of this journey added another beautiful layer to my understanding of motherhood.

To my aunt, **Laney** —
Your gentle hands pulled me from the waters of sorrow when I was barely afloat. You stepped in and became the quiet hero of my story. Your kindness, stability, and timely nudges changed everything.

To my sister, **Rachel** —
Your quiet strength is calming, steady, deeply rooted, and often expressed through your actions rather than words. You lead by example, (I always wanted to be the type of mom I saw you be), you are composed under pressure, and radiate confidence without needing to command attention. Your optimism is a light I return to often. You remind me, by simply being you, that anything is possible if you stay positive and just do it.

To my first test at parenting, my niece, **Ashley** —
Your "family first" heart, your love and support continue to be a beautiful part of my motherhood journey.

To my aunt, **Freda** —
Thank you for leading by example and for the unwavering support you've shown me and my children in every season of our lives. From braiding my daughters' hair, to patiently teaching me how to braid, to simply showing up when it mattered most on this motherhood journey — your love has always been present in both the quiet and the monumental moments. Your hands, your wisdom, and your willingness to step in without hesitation helped carry me in ways words can hardly capture. I am deeply grateful for the foundation of strength, care, and family you continue to model for us

all. Not to be taken lightly, she has given me some of the best cousins!! **(IYKYK)**

Tiersa —
Through 25+ years of friendship, highs and lows, ups and downs, you've never stopped believing in me. Your love and your unwavering vision of who I am continue to lift me higher than I dare to go on my own. You are a gift.

Romy —
To my A1 Day1— the one who stepped in at the very last minute and helped push this project across the finish line. We go way back, and somehow every time we reunite it feels like no time has passed at all. You are a walking firecracker, a loving instigator, and yes — you give me grief every single time we share space... but life would be far too quiet (and far less exciting) without you in it. Thank you for showing up, stepping up, and reminding me why our kind of friendship is rare and irreplaceable.

Robin —
My friend, who is a mother of boys *only*, some of the best advice for raising my girls came from you. Your wisdom and support know no bounds — you get it, even though the stories differ.

To my friends, some old, some new, who believed in me and continue to do so:
Too many to name, but you know who you are.

Your confidence in my voice gave it wings. Thank you for your constant presence and pure support.

Afini —
Thank you for believing I could complete this project and challenging me to **"just start".**

Synitta —
Never too busy for a call, always offering perspective, raw emotion, and honest truth, with creative reassurances — no matter the time or place. Your presence has been both an anchor and an inspiration.

KeeKee —
Too young to be my peer, too grown to be my child, yet somehow you became both. Your role in my parenting journey has been a gift. Watching you blossom into the amazing mother you are brings me deep joy and pride.

Leah —
We started as family, and you've loved my children as your own. You've supported them as they've grown into incredible young women. You've become a true friend, showing up with a love that only sisterhood offers. I'm endlessly grateful.

Bethany
You've always treated my girls like your own, showing up with constant love and support. You are family, and I'm so thankful for your presence in our lives.

To the ones who stood in the gap —
Tiffany K, Jahnee B, and Desiree B — the middle management of my motherhood journey. You were there when I couldn't be, extensions of me, and vital to my girls' growth. You are a part of their success and my motivation.

Veronica —
Your professionalism, leadership, and belief in my dreams helped carry this one across the finish line. You shaped me long before this project began, and for that, I'm forever grateful.

Marsha —
Thank you for giving me the space to feel, to vent, to be. You permitted me to exist in the chaos of motherhood and the grace I didn't even know I needed.

To **Deepa and Sonya** —
I have only known you a short time, but thank you for seeing something in me so quickly, for pouring into me, and for becoming a new light on this writing journey. Your genuine, caring spirits have inspired me deeply. I know this is just the beginning.

My motherhood is not separate from my journey as a woman. They rise and fall together. Every lesson I've learned as a mom has deepened my understanding of myself as a woman. This book reflects that sacred intersection.

To every woman who has stood in her truth, who has poured into the next generation, who has led with strength and softness — this book speaks to you. Your influence lives in every page, every reflection, and every quiet pause between the lines.

In this chapter of my life, I've been blessed not only to mother my daughters but to mentor and uplift young women who share no bloodline with me, yet hold a place in my heart. That, too, is motherhood. That, too, is womanhood.

On this shared path, we are all mothers to the next generation — molding, shaping, encouraging, and championing a better future.

After all:
The stronger the girl, the stronger the woman.
The stronger the woman, the stronger the business.
The stronger the business, the stronger the community.
The stronger the community, the stronger the family.
And should she choose, the stronger the mom.

To every woman who has hurt, inspired, or influenced me, thank you.
Your presence on my path has helped shape the woman I am becoming.

And finally, to every phenomenal woman who's ever shared a gem, a kind word, a lesson, or a piece of herself that I've passed along to another, especially to my girls — this is for you.

You are whom I pay homage to.
Your light continues to ripple.
This collection is one echo of your impact and a reflection of your imprint on my soul.

With deep gratitude and love,
Regina Elaine

Gratitude: recognizing good things, being thankful, and changing behavior or perspective, moving beyond a simple thanks to a deeper, more integrated practice of attributing the benefits received to the shape of one's life.

**BIOGRAPHY

A proud mom, wife, sister, aunt, cousin, and friend, Regina is a woman who wears many titles with love and grace. An avid journaler, list maker, and planner, she has long turned to writing as a form of expression and release—a sacred space where her inner life can unfold freely onto the page.

As the mother of two amazing young women, her oldest, 27 years old, holds a master's degree in Journalism and works as a Junior Creative for a production company in Hollywood, CA, and her youngest, 22, is a doctorate student at Syracuse University in NY pursuing her AuD in Audiology, this project is personal.

Her first literary project, *My Hero is M.O.M., Made Of Melanin*, is a deeply personal offering rooted in her lived experience and spirit. It is a multidirectional, poetic tribute to the rich, layered experience of Black motherhood—a lyrical collection of odes, poetic reflections, and intimate narrative moments that speak to the heart of being both woman and mother.

Driven by a passion to illuminate the beauty, resilience, and duality of Black mothers, Regina writes with tenderness, fire, and a deep reverence for the women who nurture, lead, and evolve through generations. With every word, she seeks to honor the complexity of motherhood and how it intersects with womanhood, the celebration of cultural pride, and the creation of a lasting tribute that feels like art in the hands and healing for the soul.

Through *My Hero is M.O.M., Made Of Melanin*, Regina invites readers to sit at the table of shared experience—a table built on love, memory, sacrifice, and becoming.

Epilogue: Black Beauty

Black Beauty

PROLOGUE:

"Black Beauty" is a new poetic expression I wrote while I was working on this project. An incident happened with my youngest daughter and her friends while out at a club. They were in a section with some young black men and my daughter and her friends were asked to leave, being told that "half of them were ugly"
While my daughter and her friends said they were not hurt by this, I was triggered and bothered, for many reasons.
My emotions were raw and open but there was nothing that I could do about it, so I wrote.

Black Beauty

Subjective and objective

Its uniqueness not respected

Unwanted opinions communicated

Self esteem deflated

Actions show, self esteem low

No repercussions for these dirty nigga discussions

The audacity to say… you ugly move out the way

Let's talk about it...

No assumptions of ignorance (on you)

Just a little deference (on me)

Help me understand

Why do you call out ugly, undefined

Ugly, undefined, means we all ugly

Yo, Momma!

Cuz I know I'm fine

All kidding aside, I say with full pride

Black girls are beautiful, we are ALL the prize

Back to yo momma

Black, beautiful in her aura

Undefined, unexplained and more

Smart, resourceful, nurturing and kind

Protective and adaptive but for her's

She don't mind

Respected and served

To those who are deserved

Lifted and bold

Our black men we hold

To expectations and protection

In public spaces and to our faces

Recognition, support and duty

With respects to our power and our beauty

Because from experience I know

This draws us to you, and the love that we show

So next time you see black women

Your opinions and fascinations

Steeped in social norms, no imagination

Do us all a favor, keep them bottled inside

Protect your moms and our culture

Display some dignity and pride

Respect black women

As a group or as one

Remember, YOU are a black woman's son

Our beauty should be

Unique and Melanated

Celebrated and Elevated

Undefined but Appreciated

Respected and Reciprocated

Black Beauty